HILLARY CLINTON

HISTORIC POLITICIAN

BY MARNE VENTURA

CONTENT CONSULTANT
Erin C. Cassese, PhD
Associate Professor & Associate Chair,
Department of Political Science, West Virginia University

Cover image: Clinton gives her concession speech on
November 9, 2016.

Core Library

An Imprint of Abdo Publishing
abdopublishing.com

abdopublishing.com

Published by Abdo Publishing, a division of ABDO, PO Box 398166, Minneapolis, Minnesota 55439. Copyright © 2018 by Abdo Consulting Group, Inc. International copyrights reserved in all countries. No part of this book may be reproduced in any form without written permission from the publisher. Core Library™ is a trademark and logo of Abdo Publishing.

Printed in the United States of America, North Mankato, Minnesota
042017
092017

Cover Photo: Matt Rourke/AP Images
Interior Photos: Matt Rourke/AP Images, 1; Rex Features/AP Images, 4–5; Bettmann/Getty Images, 7; Red Line Editorial, 8, 36; Shutterstock Images, 10, 45; Lee Balterman/The LIFE Picture Collection/Getty Images, 12–13; Wellesley College/Sygma/Getty Images, 15, 19; Charles Dixon/The Boston Globe/Getty Images, 16; Susan Adkisson/AP Images, 20–21; Amy Sancetta/AP Images, 23; Stan Honda/AFP/Getty Images, 26–27; Reuters/Alamy, 29; Evan Vucci/AFP/Getty Images, 32–33; Pete Souza/White House Photo/Getty Images, 34; Nicholas Kamm/AFP/Getty Images, 38; Krista Kennell/Shutterstock Images, 39

Editor: Heidi Schoof
Imprint Designer: Maggie Villaume
Series Design Direction: Maggie Villaume

Publisher's Cataloging-in-Publication Data

Names: Ventura, Marne, author.
Title: Hillary Clinton : historic politician / by Marne Ventura.
Other titles: Historic politician
Description: Minneapolis, MN : Abdo Publishing, 2018. | Series: Newsmakers | Includes bibliographical references and index.
Identifiers: LCCN 2017930441 | ISBN 9781532111815 (lib. bdg.) | ISBN 9781680789669 (ebook)
Subjects: LCSH: Clinton, Hillary, 1947- --Juvenile literature. | Presidents' spouses--United States--Biography--Juvenile literature. | Women cabinet officers--United States--Biography--Juvenile literature. | Cabinet officers--United States--Biography--Juvenile literature. | United States. Department of State--Biography--Juvenile literature. | Women legislators--Biography--Juvenile literature. | Legislators--Biography--Juvenile literature. | United States. Congress. Senate.--Biography--Juvenile literature. | Women Presidential candidates--United States--Biography--Juvenile literature. | Presidential candidates--United States--Biography--Juvenile literature.
Classification: DDC 973.929 [B]--dc23
LC record available at http://lccn.loc.gov/2017930441

CONTENTS

CHAPTER
ONE

HILLARY FOR PRESIDENT

Hillary Rodham Clinton stood behind the podium at a rally in Brooklyn, New York. The huge room was filled with supporters. They cheered and waved flags and signs. The date was June 6, 2016. Clinton was giving a victory speech. She had just made history. She won enough votes to be the Democratic Party candidate for US president. It would be the first time a woman had become the nominee of a major party.

Clinton thanked the people for their votes. She spoke about nearby Seneca Falls. In 1848, the first women's rights convention was held

Hillary Clinton delivers her acceptance speech at the 2016 Democratic National Convention in Philadelphia, Pennsylvania.

BECOMING A PRESIDENTIAL CANDIDATE

Every four years, Americans vote for their next president. Only one candidate from each major party runs in the November election. Others may run as independent candidates. During the first half of the year, states hold primary elections and caucuses. At these events, people vote for their favorite candidates within each party. Delegates are chosen to go to national conventions. The delegates vote to decide each party's official nominee.

there. At the time, only white men could vote. After that first meeting, activists kept fighting for equal rights. Finally, the 19th Amendment to the Constitution was passed by Congress on June 4, 1919, and ratified on August 18, 1920. It gave women the right to vote.

Clinton said she would work to make a better world for everyone. She urged the crowd to work with her. She gave her mother credit for inspiring her to serve others.

Suffragettes, who had worked to get voting rights for women, celebrated the passing of the 19th Amendment.

WOMEN IN
CONGRESS

This graph shows the percentage of women in Congress in 1965, along with the same figures in 2017. How has the makeup of Congress changed? Why do you think it has changed?

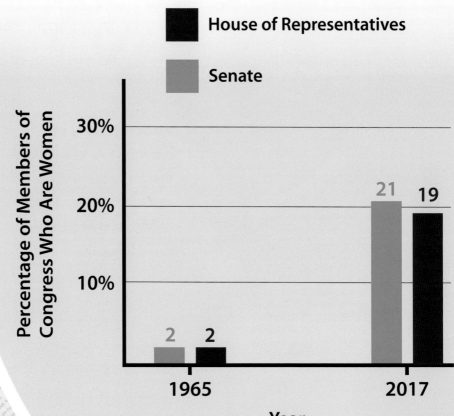

■ House of Representatives

■ Senate

Percentage of Members of Congress Who Are Women

30%

20%

21   19

10%

2   2

1965   2017

Year

BREAKING THE GLASS CEILING

The next month at the Democratic Party's national convention in Philadelphia, Pennsylvania, delegates cast their votes. Clinton's status as the Democratic Party nominee became official. On a huge screen, a video showed the faces of all of the US presidents. Next, the picture shattered into pieces. Clinton's image appeared. The crowd cheered. The video celebrated the idea of Clinton breaking the glass ceiling in politics.

Clinton has long worked to improve the lives of people in need. She has been a law professor and an attorney. She was the First Lady of Arkansas. Later she would become First Lady of the United States and

WHAT IS THE GLASS CEILING?

The glass ceiling is an invisible barrier that keeps women from succeeding as leaders and professionals. The term was first used in 1986. The *Wall Street Journal* reported that only 10 percent of senior executives were women. When a woman becomes a leader or manager, it's called breaking the glass ceiling. It means she has broken through this barrier in her career.

People used the campaign slogan "I'm with her" to express their support for Clinton in 2016.

the first female senator from New York. She was the first former First Lady to be elected senator. During President Barack Obama's first term, she served as the secretary of state. In 2016, she ran for the presidency of the United States.

STRAIGHT TO THE
SOURCE

In Clinton's victory speech, she talked about her commitment to community service and gave her mother, Dorothy Rodham, credit for teaching her this value:

> *My mother believed that life is about serving others. And she taught me never to back down from a bully, which, it turns out, was pretty good advice. This past Saturday would have been her 97th birthday, because she was born on June 4th, 1919. And some of you may know the significance of that date. On the very day my mother was born in Chicago, Congress was passing the 19th Amendment to the Constitution. That amendment finally gave women the right to vote. And I really wish my mother could be here tonight . . . I wish she could see her daughter become the Democratic Party's nominee for president of the United States.*

> Source: Katie Reilly. "Read Hillary Clinton's Historic Victory Speech as Presumptive Democratic Nominee." *Time*. Time, June 8, 2016. Web. Accessed January 30, 2017.

What's the Big Idea?

Read the excerpt from Clinton's victory speech carefully. What was Dorothy Rodham's influence on her daughter? Name two or three values that Clinton learned from her mother.

CHAPTER TWO

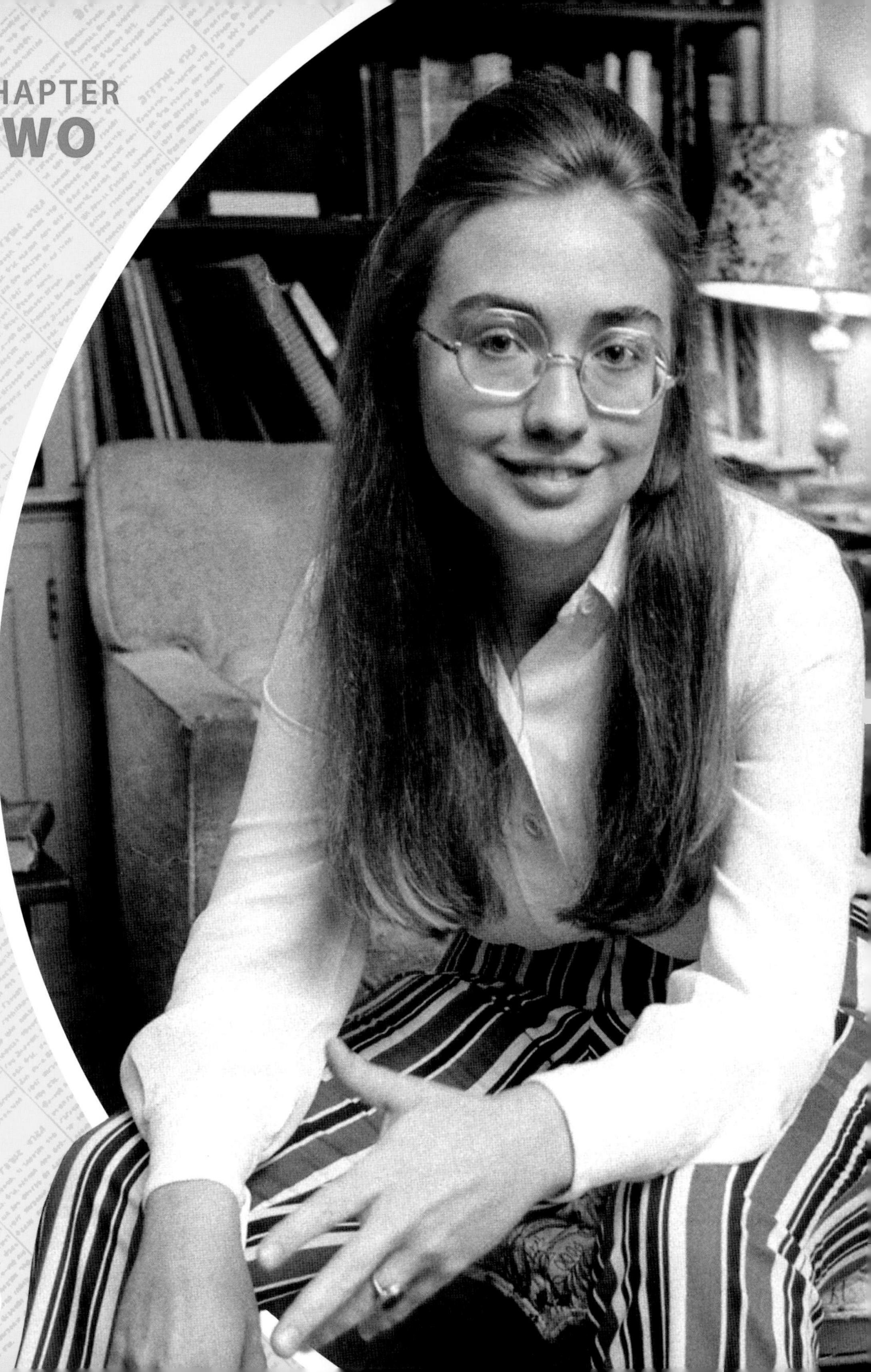

CHILDHOOD AND EDUCATION

Hillary Diane Rodham was born on October 26, 1947, in Chicago, Illinois. Her father, Hugh, owned a small drapery company. Her mother, Dorothy, was a homemaker. Hillary had two younger brothers, Hugh Jr. and Anthony. The Rodham family lived in a nice neighborhood called Park Ridge. Hugh expected his children to behave and do well in school. Dorothy taught them that with hard work, they could achieve any goal.

As president of the Wellesley College Government Association, Hillary Rodham supported student protests against the Vietnam War and social injustice.

Hillary was an excellent student. She played sports and joined Brownie and Girl Scout troops. At the age of 12, she organized backyard games to raise money for people in need. At 13, she dreamed of becoming an astronaut. Hillary was active in her church. With her youth group, she volunteered in poor neighborhoods. She also began to develop an interest in politics. In high school she was on a debating team. She was elected junior class vice president.

Next Hillary attended Wellesley, a women's college in

HILLARY AND THE SPACE RACE

In 1957, the Soviet Union launched the first spacecraft into Earth orbit. The US space program competed with that of the Soviet Union. When 13-year-old Hillary learned about the space race, she wanted to help. She wrote a letter to the National Aeronautics and Space Administration (NASA) and asked how she could become an astronaut. NASA sent Hillary a reply, but its letter was a disappointment. It said they didn't accept women. It wasn't until 1978, 21 years later, that NASA hired its first female astronauts.

Hillary graduated from Maine South High School in Park Ridge, Illinois, in 1965.

Massachusetts. Hillary and many of her fellow students were unhappy with injustice in society. American soldiers were fighting in the Vietnam War (1954–1975). Many people were opposed to the war.

Hillary's mother was a Democrat. Her father was a Republican. In high school and in her early college years, Hillary was active in Republican politics. She was

Hillary, *in white, on left of second row,* participated in the procession of graduates to the commencement ceremony as a junior at Wellesley College in 1968.

the head of the Young Republicans Club in 1966. She worked as an intern in Washington, DC, for the House Republican Conference in 1968. As she learned more about politics, Hillary decided to switch to the Democratic Party. She worked as a volunteer for Eugene McCarthy. He was an antiwar candidate for president. In her senior year of college, she was elected student body president.

Before 1969, only administrators or guest speakers gave speeches at Wellesley graduation ceremonies. The year of Hillary's graduation, students persuaded the school to let students have a voice. They chose Hillary to be their speaker. Before Hillary's speech, a Republican senator spoke. He urged students not to protest against America's problems. When it was Hillary's turn to talk, she disagreed with the senator. She advised her peers to speak up for a better world. Her audience stood up and clapped.

POLITICAL PARTIES

A political party is a group of people who share ideas about how government should work. In the United States, the two biggest parties are the Democratic and Republican Parties. Both want what is best for the country. But they often disagree about how this should be done. In general, Democrats think government should do more to help people. Republicans want less government. They feel that people should do things for themselves. Other political parties include the Green Party and the Libertarian Party.

GRADUATE SCHOOL AND CHILDREN'S RIGHTS

After Wellesley, Hillary went to Yale Law School in Connecticut. While at Yale, Hillary decided to focus on family law and voting rights. During school breaks, she helped children in Florida get health care and schooling. She also helped African Americans and Latinos register to vote in Texas. She worked for the Children's Defense Fund to solve problems that kept children from going to school. Hillary graduated in 1973 with honors. That year she met Bill Clinton, also a law student. They started dating. Hillary stayed at Yale while Bill finished school.

On October 11, 1975, the couple married. Both became law professors at the University of Arkansas. The following year, Bill was elected Arkansas attorney general. The couple moved to Little Rock, the state's capital. Soon after, Hillary worked for Democratic presidential candidate Jimmy Carter's campaign.

Because she and Bill were active in politics, reporters and community members noticed Hillary.

Young Bill Clinton bought a house in Fayetteville, Arkansas, to give Hillary more reason to accept his marriage proposal. The wedding took place at their new home.

Often they criticized her for not acting like a traditional woman. She didn't change her name to Clinton right away after her marriage. She still called herself Hillary Rodham. Later she began going by the name Hillary Rodham Clinton. She wore thick glasses. She didn't style her curly hair, wear makeup, or paint her nails. These things were not as important to her as her work.

CHAPTER
THREE

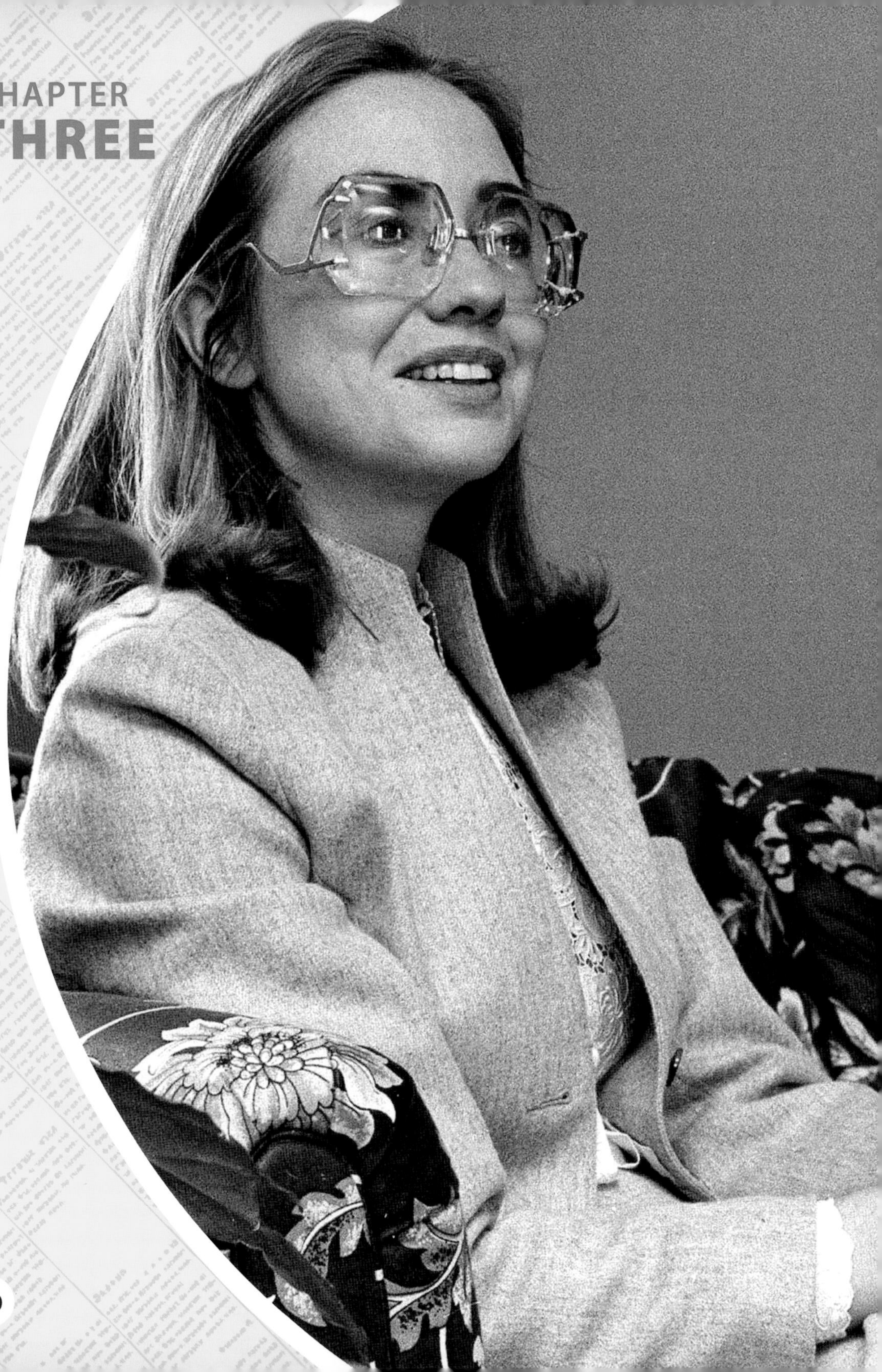

FIRST LADY

n 1976, the Rose Law Firm hired Clinton. It was the first time the 156-year-old firm had hired a female lawyer. Two years later, Bill was elected governor of Arkansas. Clinton became the state's First Lady. In 1980, their daughter, Chelsea, was born. During this time, Clinton worked on programs to help children and the needy. In 1988 and 1991 she made the list of the nation's 100 most influential lawyers.

In 1992, Bill ran for president of the United States and won. The Clintons moved to Washington, DC. During the election, Bill told Americans they would get a two-for-one deal if they elected him. Clinton would help run the country, too. Bill put her in

By 1983, Hillary Rodham Clinton was a mother, a successful lawyer, and the First Lady of Arkansas.

FIRST LADY

Historians don't know exactly when or why Americans started calling the president's wife the First Lady. Some say the title was given to President James Madison's wife, Dolley. The term was widely used in most US newspapers by the 1870s. There is no official definition of the First Lady's role. All have served as hostesses at White House functions. Many have done charity work. They may be champions of a special cause. Eleanor Roosevelt was one of the most active first ladies. She worked as an advocate for the needy and for civil and women's rights. Clinton admired Eleanor Roosevelt. She tried to follow Roosevelt's example when she became First Lady.

charge of studying new health-care plans. Clinton set up an office in the White House. Many people thought it was not her place to work on health care. They thought she should act more like a traditional First Lady.

WOMEN'S RIGHTS AROUND THE WORLD

Clinton was disappointed. But she soon found a new cause. She began to travel to

President Bill Clinton hugs Hillary and Chelsea after taking the oath of office in 1993.

other countries. Clinton visited places where women didn't have the same rights as men. In some countries, women and girls couldn't get an education. Clinton wanted to help make the world a safe, fair place for all people. She went to a United Nations meeting in Beijing, China, in 1995. Members of the president's staff warned Clinton not to offend Chinese officials by criticizing them. Clinton spoke up anyway. She pointed out ways that women were not treated fairly in China and other parts of Asia. She said, "Women's rights are human rights, once and for all." The Chinese government wouldn't let reports of

WHAT ARE HUMAN RIGHTS?

The United Nations is an organization that promotes human rights around the world. When it was founded in 1945, First Lady Eleanor Roosevelt and a group of leaders from other countries wrote a list of freedoms that all people should have. These human rights include the right to life, privacy, education, travel, food, clothing, housing, medical care, and free speech.

her speech be printed in their newspapers. But it made
front-page news in the rest of the world. Some people
say it was the most important speech of Clinton's career.

FURTHER EVIDENCE

This chapter tells about Clinton's work as First Lady of Arkansas
and of the United States. What is one of the chapter's main
points? What key evidence supports this point? Take a look at
the article on the website below. It gives information about
Clinton's accomplishments during this time. Does the website
support the main points in this chapter? Write a few sentences
using new information from the website as evidence to support
a point in the chapter.

WHITE HOUSE HISTORICAL ASSOCIATION:
HILLARY CLINTON
abdocorelibrary.com/hillary-clinton

CHAPTER
FOUR

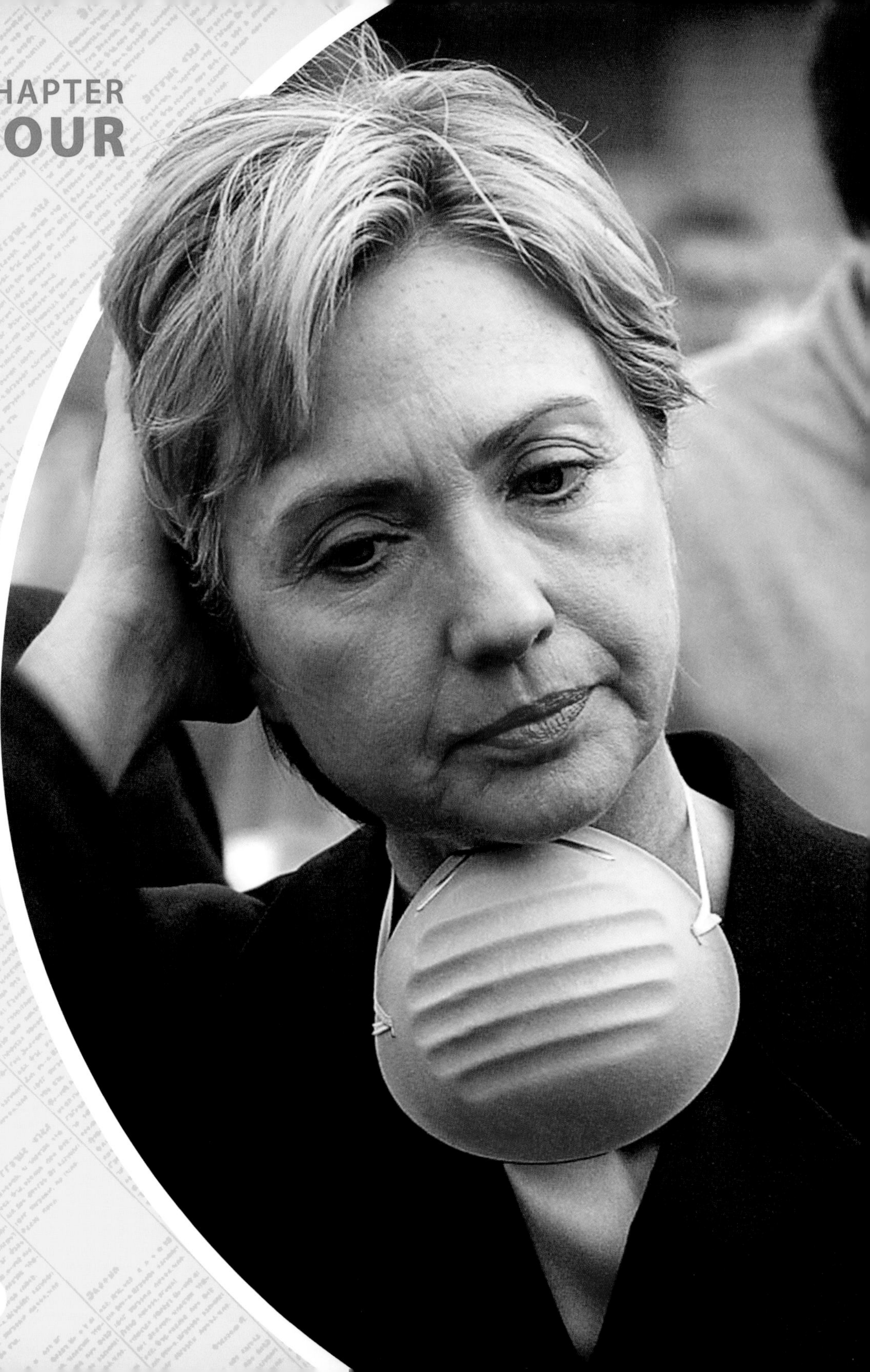

SENATOR HILLARY CLINTON

B ill's second term as president ended in 2001. Clinton wanted her own career in politics, so she decided to run for senator from New York the previous fall. Clinton began to travel around the state. She met with New Yorkers in cities, in small towns, and on farms. Clinton won the election.

On September 11, 2001, terrorists flew jets into the World Trade Center towers in New York City. They destroyed both skyscrapers and killed almost 3,000 Americans. Afterward,

US Senator Hillary Clinton toured the damage in lower Manhattan one day after the September 11, 2001, terrorist attacks.

THE UNITED STATES SENATE

Two senators are elected from each of the 50 United States. They serve for six-year terms. Senators work with members of the House of Representatives to propose, write, and vote on laws. They also have to vote on whether to approve some of the president's decisions. Together, the Senate and House of Representatives are called Congress. They make up the legislative branch of government.

Clinton worked to help victims. The attack released toxic fumes. The air was unhealthy for workers clearing the rubble. Clinton raised awareness and money to help clean up the air and provide medical help for sick workers.

FIRST RUN FOR PRESIDENT

During her time as a New York senator, Clinton worked for health-care reform and children's rights. She worked to make life better for veterans and their families. She was re-elected in 2006.

In 2007, Clinton made her first run for president of the United States. She competed with Barack Obama to

US Senators Hillary Clinton and Barack Obama participate in a Democratic Party debate during the 2008 presidential campaign.

become the Democratic Party's nominee. Obama was a senator from Illinois. Both were historic candidates. If she won, Clinton would become the first female major party nominee. If he won, Obama would become the first black major party nominee.

For much of the race, Clinton and Obama were very close in the polls. It seemed that they had an equal chance of winning. Both won about 18 million votes in the primaries. Clinton won in California and

ELECTORAL COLLEGE

The system the US government uses to elect a president is called the Electoral College. Each state chooses a certain number of electors. The number is based on the population of the state. States with more people have more electors. When people vote for a presidential candidate, their votes are counted. This is called the popular vote. In most states, all the electors are awarded to the candidate who wins the popular vote in that state. This system makes it possible for a candidate who wins the national popular vote to lose the election. Some people think the Electoral College should be abolished. Others believe it is a good system.

New York. But Obama won more total states and delegate votes. He became the 2008 Democratic Party nominee.

Obama went on to run against John McCain in the general election. McCain was a Republican senator from Arizona. Obama won a strong victory. He got the largest percentage of the popular vote for a Democrat since 1964. In the Electoral College, he got 365 votes to McCain's 173.

STRAIGHT TO THE
SOURCE

Dan Balz, a writer for the *Washington Post*, talks about Clinton's decision to run for president in the 2008 election:

> *Clinton brings considerable assets to the race. As a former first lady now serving her second term in the Senate, she has one of the best-known names in American politics. She has a national network of supporters, the capacity to raise as much or more money than any of her rivals, and a résumé of political activity dating back decades that now includes six years in the Senate and a landslide reelection victory in November. And for the past 15 years, she has shown an ability to weather sometimes harsh attacks from her critics, especially among conservatives.*

> Source: Dan Balz. "Hillary Clinton Opens Presidential Bid." Washington Post. *Washington Post*, January 21, 2007. Web. Accessed January 30, 2017.

Back It Up

The author of this passage is using evidence to support a point. Write a paragraph describing the point the author is making. Then write down two or three pieces of evidence the author uses to make the point.

CHAPTER FIVE

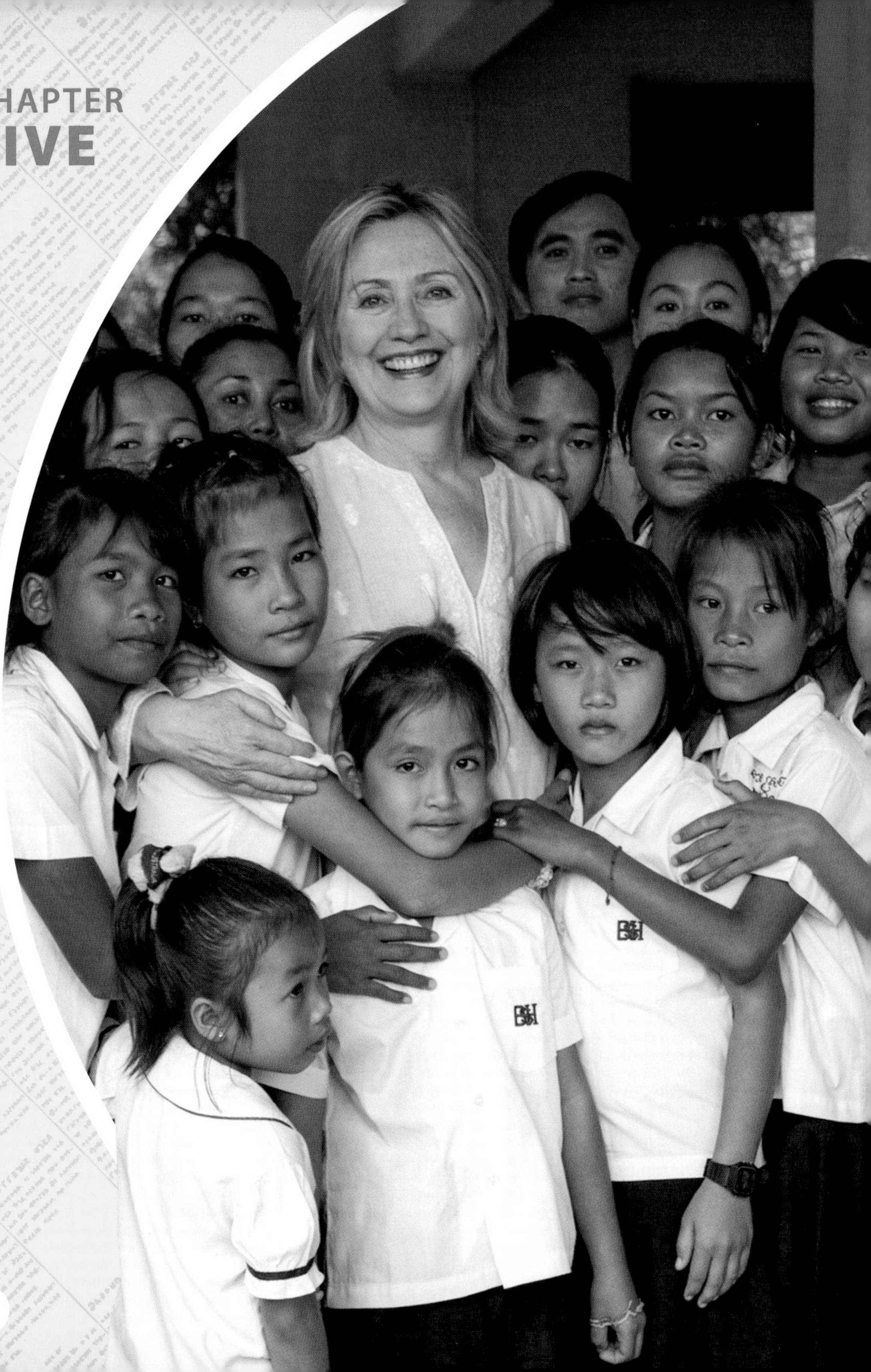

SECRETARY OF STATE AND THE 2016 ELECTION

When Barack Obama became president of the United States in 2009, he asked Clinton to be his secretary of state. She accepted. Clinton served from 2009 to 2013. She was the only former First Lady to become a secretary of state.

During her four years of service, Clinton visited 112 countries. She used her skills and

US Secretary of State Clinton poses with children during a tour of the Siem Reap shelter in Cambodia.

As secretary of state, Clinton participated in national security meetings in the Situation Room.

experience to help find solutions to global problems. US soldiers still fought in Iraq and Afghanistan. Terrorists were still a threat. Some governments in the Middle East were unstable.

Clinton called her plan for the United States to deal with foreign countries *smart power*. The idea was to avoid the use of military force. Instead the United States would use diplomacy and help countries develop their economies. She also called for sanctions, or penalties, to stop countries from developing nuclear weapons.

Clinton met with world leaders to find ways to slow climate change and save Earth's environment. She visited family and women's rights activists around the world too. She wanted to help give women and children a fair chance at a good education, health care, and other rights.

In September 2012, four Americans working in Benghazi, Libya, were killed. The Americans were there to help Libyans build a democracy. After the incident, some people

SECRETARY OF STATE

The US president chooses the secretary of state with the approval of the Senate. This person's job is to advise the president about foreign countries. The secretary also meets with foreign leaders to make agreements. The secretary helps the president choose ambassadors. She or he oversees the safety of Americans in foreign countries.

CLINTON'S
TRAVELS AS SECRETARY
OF STATE

As secretary of state, Clinton visited a record 112 countries in four years. These countries are shaded on this map. From the map below, identify a country that Clinton visited. What kinds of issues might she have discussed with representatives from that country?

Countries visited

blamed Clinton for not doing a better job of protecting the Americans.

THE CAMPAIGN

After President Obama was re-elected in 2012, he asked Clinton to stay on as secretary of state. But Clinton said no. She was happy to have served the country for four years. Now she was ready for a new job. In April 2015, Clinton announced that she was going to run for president again.

Newspapers began to report that Clinton had used a private e-mail account to send and receive messages while she was secretary of state. Critics claimed this was a problem because she was supposed to use a secure government server. Enemies from other countries might be able to hack a private account. Clinton was investigated for wrongdoing. In July 2015, investigators decided she was not guilty of any crime. Clinton apologized for using a private e-mail server.

2016 Democratic presidential nominee Hillary Clinton thanks her supporters on the final day of the Democratic National Convention.

Many voters still blamed her. They felt she had shown bad judgment.

Soon Clinton was the Democratic Party nominee. Her opponent was Republican Donald Trump. Unlike Clinton, Trump had no experience in politics or public service. He was a wealthy businessman who owned a group of hotels and casinos. He was also a reality television star. Trump was at the center of many scandals. In one, a tape recording showed him

Clinton has been a role model for her daughter, Chelsea, and for other young women to get involved and work to make the world a better place.

making crude comments about women. Most polls and newspaper reports gave Clinton a high chance of winning the election.

Eleven days before the election, the head of the Federal Bureau of Investigation (FBI) sent a letter to Congress. He said the agency had found more of Clinton's e-mails and might reopen its investigation. A few days later, he said the investigation would not be reopened. But the news caused many voters

CONCESSION SPEECH

When enough votes have been counted to confirm that one candidate has won the election, the losing candidate usually calls the opponent to offer congratulations. Then she or he makes a public concession speech. Modern technology such as computers, television, and the Internet allow Americans to know results immediately. In past elections, losing candidates announced their congratulations by letter, telegram, or radio. Traditionally, a concession speech urges Americans to work together and support the new president-elect.

to suspect Clinton had indeed done something wrong.

MOVING FORWARD

On Election Day, Clinton won the popular vote by approximately 2.8 million votes. However, Trump won more Electoral College votes. He had won the election.

It was a big disappointment for Clinton. But she urged her supporters not to give up. In her concession speech, she said, "To all the little girls who are watching this, never doubt that you are valuable and powerful and deserving of every chance and opportunity in the world to pursue and achieve your own dreams." She went on to say, "So now, our responsibility as citizens is to keep doing our part to build that better, stronger, fairer America we seek."

Clinton has been a champion of equal rights for women, children, families, and the needy for most of her life. She hasn't let setbacks stop her from working for a better America. From her early days as a lawyer to her presidential campaigns, she has dedicated her life to public service.

EXPLORE ONLINE

Chapter Five discusses Clinton's concession speech following the 2016 election. The article below includes the transcript of the speech. Is the information given on the website different from the information in this chapter? How is it the same? How do the two sources present information differently?

HILLARY CLINTON'S CONCESSION SPEECH
abdocorelibrary.com/hillary-clinton

IMPORTANT
DATES

1947
Hillary Diane Rodham is born on October 26 in Chicago, Illinois.

1969
Hillary graduates from Wellesley College.

1973
Hillary graduates from Yale Law School.

1973
Hillary works at Children's Defense Fund in Massachusetts.

1975
Hillary and Bill Clinton are married.

1976
Clinton becomes the first female partner at Rose Law Firm.

1979–1981 and 1983–1992
Clinton is First Lady of Arkansas.

1993–2001
Clinton is First Lady of the United States.

2000
Clinton is elected senator from New York.

2009–2013
Clinton serves as President Barack Obama's secretary of state.

2016
Clinton is nominated as the Democratic candidate for president.

2016
Clinton loses the presidential election to Republican Donald Trump.

STOP AND
THINK

Tell the Tale

Chapter One of this book describes the rally where Clinton celebrated becoming the Democratic candidate for US president. Imagine you have a sister who hopes to run for president one day. Write a 200-word letter to her describing the rally. How did Hillary's victory pave the way for more girls to enter politics?

Take a Stand

Clinton often spoke out against the advice of others. At her graduation from Wellesley, the senator who spoke before her stated his belief that students should not actively protest the government. When it was Clinton's turn to speak, she told the audience that she disagreed with the senator. When she was First Lady of the United States, she criticized the Chinese government for not treating women fairly. Do you think it was helpful for Clinton to publicly disagree with the senator and foreign leaders? Or do you think it was inappropriate? Give reasons for your opinion.

Dig Deeper

After reading this book, what questions do you still have about Clinton? With an adult's help, find a few reliable sources that can help you answer your questions. Write a paragraph about what you learned.

Why Do I Care?

Americans under the age of 18 are not allowed to vote in a presidential election. But that doesn't mean you can't think about how you would vote. Why is it important to learn about how elections work? What sources can you use to find out about the different candidates? Why is it important to vote once you're old enough?

GLOSSARY

activists
people who work for change

advocate
a person who argues for
a cause

candidate
a person who runs for office

climate change
the change in Earth's
temperature caused by the
release of greenhouse gases
into the atmosphere

convention
a meeting of people for a
special purpose, sometimes
to make an official decision

delegates
people who are chosen to
vote or act for others

influential
having power to
control something

nominee
a person chosen as
a candidate

server
a computer that manages
access to a network

volunteer
a person who chooses to
work without being paid

LEARN
MORE

Books

Alexander, Heather. *Who Is Hillary Clinton?* New York:
    Grosset & Dunlap, 2016.

Cunningham, Kevin. *How Political Campaigns
    and Elections Work.* Minneapolis, MN: Abdo
    Publishing, 2015.

Levinson, Cynthia. *Hillary Rodham Clinton: Do All the Good
    You Can.* New York: Balzer & Bray, 2016.

Websites

To learn more about Newsmakers, visit **abdobooklinks.com**.
These links are routinely monitored and updated to provide
the most current information available.

Visit **abdocorelibrary.com** for free additional tools for
teachers and students.

INDEX

About the Author

Marne Ventura is the author of many children's books, both fiction and nonfiction. Her favorite topics include science, technology, arts and crafts, and the lives of creative people.